PARTY TIME!

It's Charlie Caterpillar's birthday!
Help him get his party started by completing
all the unfinished shapes and patterns.

GOAL:
to recognize patterns,
shapes and colors

CAN YOU SPOT...
1 sun • 2 rabbits • 3 owls •
4 butterflies • 5 birds?

GOAL:
to count to 5

READY, SET, GO!
These frosty friends are having a race.
Listen carefully as a grown-up reads
the instructions, and guide each animal
to the correct lane.

Mr. Fox is skating in lane 3.

The winner is finishing in lane 4.

Ms. Polar Bear is skating in the lane next to the winner.

Mr. Rabbit is skating in lane 1.

Ms. Cat's lane is in between Mr. Fox's and Mr. Rabbit's.

WHO IS THE WINNER?

1 2 3 4 5

HOW MANY CAN YOU COUNT?
Toys: ...
Fruit: ...
Clothes: ...
Vehicles: ...

GOAL:
to classify objects

LET IT SNOW

Trace over the dotted lines and color in the drawing to bring Snowy to life!

ALL IN A ROW

The farmer wants to have one of each animal in every row. Four animals still need to find their place. Draw a line from each animal at the top to the right spot in the table.

GOAL:
to read a table and to think logically

DINNER TIME

Color in all the things that can be eaten.
Which is your favorite?

A HEALTHY SNACK

Put these scenes in the right order.
What happens first gets number 1,
what happens last gets number 3.
Write the numbers inside the flowers.

GOAL:
to think logically

LITTLE AND LARGE

Put the turtles in the correct order from small to big by drawing a line from each turtle to the correct flower below.

MUSIC IS MY FIRST LOVE!

These virtuosos love playing their instruments. Join in by tracing over the dotted lines.

GOAL:
to develop manual dexterity

CLUCK, CLUCK, CLUCK

The hen laid lots of eggs. Now the egg cartons can be filled. Connect each box to the number of eggs needed to fill it.

GOAL: to add up to 6

ODD SOCKS

All the socks have been mixed up!
Can you find the pairs?
Draw lines to connect
the matching socks.

GOAL:
to recognize patterns,
shapes and colors

WOOLLY ALPACA

Color the soft blanket in the right colors. Look carefully at the sequence of colors and complete the pattern.

GOAL: to complete color sequences

ANIMAL GATHERINGS

How many animals are in each picture?
Connect each picture with
the correct number.

GOAL:
to count and
to recognize
numbers

3

2

1

WHO'S THE HEAVIEST?
Color the heaviest animal in blue.
Color the lightest animal in red.

GOAL:
to understand
the concept
of weight

BEST FRIENDS

Draw a circle around
each group of two animals.

GOAL:
to count to 4

HOME SWEET HOME

Where do these animals live?
Connect each animal to its home.

HOME

SHAPE CIRCUS

Color all the squares red, all the triangles blue and all the circles yellow.

PAINTS AND SHAPES

Look at the colors at the top of this table and the shapes to the left. Complete the table with the right shapes in the right colors.

GOAL:
to read a table and to think logically

TWIN TIGERS

Can you spot the twins?
Connect each tiger with its twin.

GOAL:
to recognize
similarities and
differences

YUMMY!
These friends are looking for their favorite snacks. Follow the lines and discover which animal gets which treat. The colors and letters may give you a clue!

GOAL:
to develop manual dexterity and to recognize letters

A   B   C   D

A

D

C

B

I'M HERE!

Ask a grown-up to read these sentences carefully. Can you find the animals they are talking about?

GOAL:
to think logically

Stella has more kittens than Lily.

Billie the butterfly has a striped belly. She is smaller than her sister.

Hugo the dog has a gray spot around his eye.

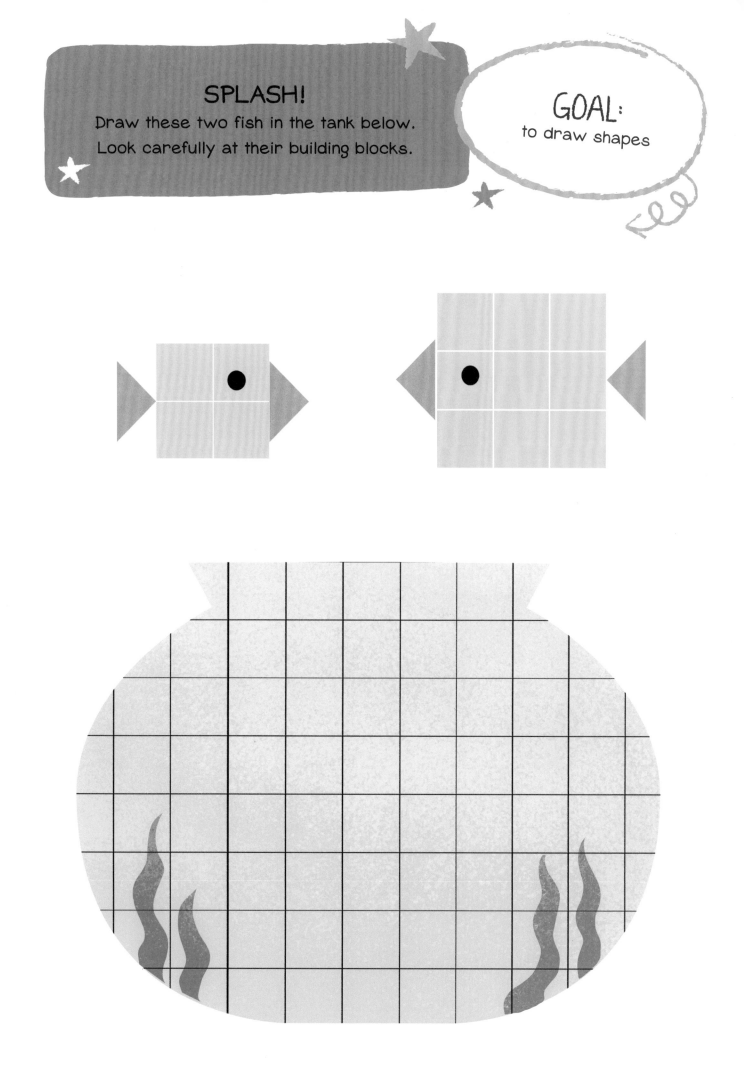

UNDER THE STARS

Little Bear loves camping!
Finish this picture by tracing
over the dotted lines.

GOAL:
to develop
manual dexterity

TASTY SOUP

These chefs are busy making soup.
Which pot is the fullest? Color in that spoon.
Then color in the tallest chef's hat.

GOAL:
to make comparisons
and to understand the
concepts of "fullest"
and "tallest"

GIFT SHOPPING
Put these scenes in the right order.
What happens first gets number 1,
what happens last gets number 4.

GOAL:
to think logically

LAUNDRY DAY

The laundry has been hung out to dry in the warm sun. Count the clothes on each clothesline. Write the number in the blue circle.

GOAL: to count to 7

DEEP BLUE SEA
Some of these things don't belong underwater. Cross them out.

GOAL:
to make associations

COUNT AND COLOR
Color all the frogs green, all the owls purple and all the cats orange. Count how many there are of each and write the numbers in the flowers.

GOAL:
to count to 5

.... CATS

.... OWLS

.... FROGS

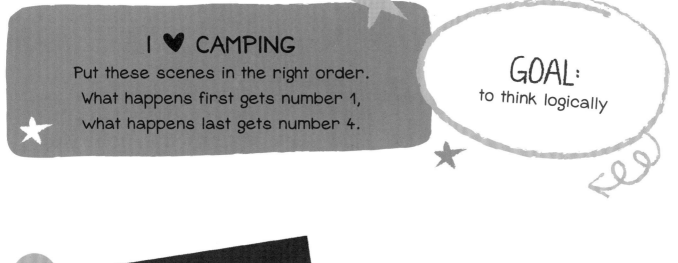

I ♥ CAMPING

Put these scenes in the right order.
What happens first gets number 1,
what happens last gets number 4.

GOAL:
to think logically

FARMER FRANK
Color in all the things
that belong on a farm.

GOAL:
to make associations

A DASH OF COLOR

Color in 1 horse, 2 frogs, 3 sheep, 4 trees and 5 chickens.

GOAL: to count to 5

MIRROR, MIRROR ON THE WALL

Find the mirror image of each animal.
Circle each pair in a different color.

ODD ONE OUT

In each row, there is one object that doesn't belong. Circle it.

WHAT'S WRONG?

Ask a grown-up to read the sentence next to each picture. Listen carefully: there's something wrong. What is it?

GOAL: to practice listening comprehension

Rosie Rabbit has more carrots than Cedric Cat.

Penny Penguin is enjoying a ride on the sled.

Birdie sits on the tallest cactus.

Dean Dog has a bigger ice-cream cone than Millie Mouse.

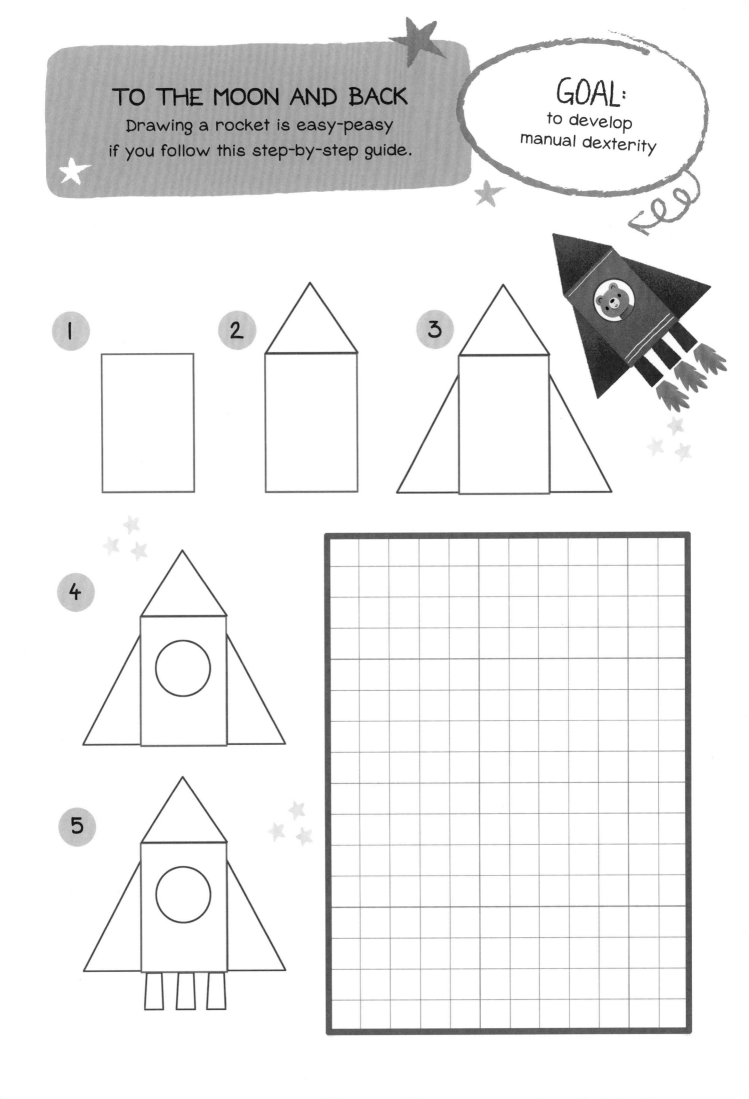

TO THE MOON AND BACK

Drawing a rocket is easy-peasy
if you follow this step-by-step guide.

GOAL: to develop manual dexterity

1

2

3

4

5

BEST FRIENDS

Make groups of 2 crocodiles by drawing a circle around each pair. How many groups do you have? Color in the right number.

SNOW CAT

Put these scenes in the right order.
What happens first gets number 1,
what happens last gets number 4.

GOAL:
to think logically

SPOTS AND STRIPES

In the top row, each ball has a unique pattern and color. Every row below should contain the same 4 patterns. Color in the blank ones.

GOAL: to recognize and reproduce patterns

HAPPY HOBBIES

Discover every animal's favorite activity.
Connect the images that belong together.

GOAL:
to make associations

OVER THE RAINBOW

Sparkle Unicorn wants to reach
the rainbow. Can you take her there?

ABC, 123

Mr. Fox has written letters and numbers on the board. Color in the numbers. Do not color in the letters.

MATCH THE SHADOWS
Connect each animal to its own shadow.

GOAL: to recognize similarities and differences

PERFECTLY SHAPED
Give every shape the same color
as its matching object.

GOAL:
to recognize shapes
and colors